IL TROVATORE

Opera in Four Acts

Music by
Giuseppe Verdi

Libretto by
SALVATORE CAMMARANO

English Version by
BERNARD STAMBLER

Ed. 2537

G. SCHIRMER, Inc.

DISTRIBUTED BY
HAL•LEONARD®
CORPORATION
7777 W. BLUEMOUND RD. P.O. BOX 13819 MILWAUKEE, WI 53213

The first performance using this translation of *Il Trovatore* took place on July 6, 1963, at the Central City Opera House, Central City, Colorado.

Note

G. SCHIRMER, INC.

IL TROVATORE

In April 1851, just after the triumphant premiere of *Rigoletto,* Verdi began a correspondence with Salvatore Cammarano to discuss an opera based on Antonio García Guitiérrez' *El Trovador,* a play at the moment highly successful in Madrid. Cammarano, who had provided Verdi with the librettos for *Alzira,* the *Battaglia di Legnano,* and *Luisa Miller* (he also wrote the libretto for Donizetti's *Lucia di Lammermoor*), was a somewhat Byronic Neapolitan poet who shared certain concepts about opera with Richard Wagner. He wrote, in a letter to Verdi:

"Did I not fear to be branded as an Utopian, I should be tempted to say that for an opera to obtain the maximum of perfection, one mind should be responsible for both text and music. From this it will be clear that when two authors are involved, I think that the least they can do is to collaborate with the greatest possible intimacy. Poetry should be neither the slave nor the tyrant of music."

Verdi's collaboration with Cammarano was disturbed—or possibly deepened— by personal tragedy: in June of 1851 his mother died. Verdi had been originally attracted to Guitiérrez' play by the character of Azucena (and at one point considered naming the opera after her); his deep attachment to his mother may be indirectly responsible for the intensity of Azucena's music.

A draft of the libretto was ready in the spring of 1852; by September the libretto was nearly complete, although Cammarano died before the last revisions were made and the poet Leone Emanuele completed the task. Verdi may well have been thinking in musical terms while discussing the libretto with Cammarano, but he actually wrote the music for *Il Trovatore* between the 1st and the 29th of November 1852.

Roman audiences attending the first performance, on January 19, 1853, had to wade through mud and water to enter the Apollo Theater because the Tiber had overflowed its banks. The inconvenience was forgotten, however, by the time the curtain fell; both the third-act finale and the entire fourth act had to be repeated. The opera made its American bow on May 2, 1855, at the New York Academy of Music and reached the Metropolitan on the third night of its inaugural season in 1883.

THE STORY

ACT I (The Duel). In the guardroom of Count Di Luna's apartments in the palace of Aliaferia in fifteenth-century Aragon, the men are on watch to apprehend a wandering troubadour, Manrico, who as a rival to the Count has been serenading the noble Leonora. The captain, Ferrando, keeps his men awake by telling the story of a gipsy who was burned to death for bewitching the Count's younger brother as a child. Her daughter, Azucena, avenged herself by abducting the boy and is thought to have burned him at the same stake where the mother perished, but the Count still searches for him.

In the palace garden, the Lady Leonora tells her companion Ines how, at a tournament, she first saw a strange knight in black armor, placed the laurel wreath on his brow and then beheld him no more until the quiet evening that he first came as a troubadour to serenade her. Although Ines confesses misgivings, her mistress declares love for the stranger. No sooner have the women entered the palace than Count Di Luna appears, but before he can follow them Manrico's song is heard. When Leonora, rushing out, betrays her preference for the troubadour, the Count in a jealous rage challenges him to a duel. She swoons as they hurry away.

ACT II (The Gipsy). As dawn breaks over their camp in the mountains of Biscay, the gipsies sing, take up their hammers and set to work. Suddenly Azucena describes the fiery scene of her mother's execution and calls for vengeance. As the band disperses, Manrico, who is recuperating from his duel with the Count, remains to question the old woman on his parentage; she lets slip that it was her own child whom she hurled into the flames by mistake, but insists that she has given Manrico a mother's love. When Azucena asks why he spared Di Luna during the duel, the troubadour replies that a mysterious power stayed his hand. He rushes off, over her protest, on learning that Leonora is about to take the veil.

At the convent cloister where Leonora, believing Manrico dead, plans to retire, the Count prepares to kidnap her. He cannot bear to live without her. At the last moment, Manrico intervenes; his forces overcome Di Luna's and he escapes with Leonora, who is overjoyed that her lover still lives.

ACT III (The Gipsy's Son). The Count has pitched his camp near the castle of Castellor, now held by Manrico, who has taken Leonora there. As Di Luna's soldiers sing of their eagerness for victory, Ferrando drags in Azucena, whom he has found lurking nearby. She describes her lonely life and tells them she is trying to locate her son; the Count torments her into admitting that it is Manrico and orders her to the stake.

Within the castle, Manrico comforts Leonora on the day of their wedding, but the ceremonies are rudely interrupted by Ruiz with news that Azucena has been captured. The son stares in horror at his mother's pyre and vows to save her.

ACT IV (The Torture). Ruiz brings Leonora to the stronghold of Aliaferia Palace, from which she hopes to rescue Manrico, who has been caught. No sooner has she voiced her undying love for him than the solemn Miserere is heard that spells his doom, broken by the song of the troubadour himself as he longs for release in death. Leonora resolves to purchase his freedom by yielding to the Count, at whose astonished acquiescence she rejoices. Di Luna does not see her swallow poison

In their dismal cell, Azucena and Manrico dream of returning to the happy freedom of the mountains. As the old woman falls asleep, Leonora enters to announce her lover's pardon and urge him to haste, but Manrico denounces her when he learns the price. Gasping her innocence, she dies in his arms as the Count enters. In a fury he orders Manrico to the block. Azucena, roused by the troubadour's cry of farewell, staggers to the window just as he is executed. But the final triumph is hers. In wild exultation she cries that her mother is avenged: the Count has killed his own brother.

Courtesy of Opera News

CAST OF CHARACTERS

LEONORA, a noble lady of Aragon . . . . Soprano

MANRICO, a troubadour, in reality Di Luna's brother . . . . Tenor

COUNT DI LUNA, a powerful noble of the Prince of Aragon . . . . Baritone

AZUCENA, a Biscayan gipsy woman . . . . Mezzo-Soprano

FERRANDO, Di Luna's Captain of the Guard . . . . Bass

INES, Leonora's lady-in-waiting . . . . Soprano

RUIZ, a soldier in Manrico's service . . . . Tenor

A GIPSY . . . . Bass

A MESSENGER . . . . Tenor

Attendants, Soldiers, Gipsies and Nuns

PLACE: Aragon

TIME: 15th Century

SYNOPSIS OF SCENES

IL TROVATORE

ATTO PRIMO

IL DUELLO

SCENA 1

Atrio nel palazzo dell' Aliaferia; porta da un lato, che mette agli appartamenti del Conte di Luna.—Ferrando e molti famigliari del Conte, che giacciono presso la porta: alcuni uomini d' arme passeggiano in fondo.

FERRANDO

(parlando ai famigliari)

All'erta, all'erta! Il Conte n'è d'uopo
attender vigilando; ed egli talor, presso i veroni della sua cara, intere passa
le notti.

FAMIGLIARI

Gelosia le fiere serpi gli avventa in petto!

FERRANDO

Nel trovator, che dai giardini muove
notturno il canto, d'un rivale a dritto
ei teme.

FAMIGLIARI

Dalle gravi palpèbre il sonno a discac-
ciar, la vera storia ci narra di Garzia,
germano al nostro Conte.

FERRANDO

La dirò: venite intorno a me.

(Famigliari eseguiscono accostandosi pur essi.)

UOMINI D' ARME

Noi pure . . .

FAMIGLIARI *(accostandosi)*

Udite, udite.

(Tutti accerchiano Ferrando.)

FERRANDO

Di due figli vivea, padre beato,
Il buon Conte di Luna:

Fida nutrice del secondo nato
Dormia presso la cuna.
Sul romper dell' aurora un bel mattino
Ella dischiude i rai,
E chi trova d'accanto a quel bambino?

CORO

Chi? Favella, chi mai?

FERRANDO

Abbietta zingara, fosca vegliarda!
Cingeva i simboli di maliarda!
E sul fanciullo, con viso arcigno,
L'occhio affiggeva torvo, sanguigno!
D'orror compresa la nutrice;
Acuto un grido all'aura scioglie;
Ed ecco, in meno che labbro il dice
I servi accorrono in quelle soglie;
E fra minacce, urli, percosse,
La rea discacciano ch'entrarvi osò.

CORO

Giusto quei petti sdegno commosse!
L'insana vecchia lo provocò!

FERRANDO

Asserî che tirar del fanciullino
L' oroscopo volea . . .
Bugiarda!—Lenta febbre del meschino
La salute struggea!
Coverto di pallor languido, affranto
Ei tremava la sera!
Il dì traeva in lamentevol pianto,

1

IL TROVATORE

ACT I

THE DUEL

SCENE I

A vestibule in the palace of Aliaferia; on one side is a door which leads to the quarters of the Count Di Luna. Ferrando and several servants of the Count are lounging near the door; several soldiers are standing watch nearby.

FERRANDO
(speaking to the servants)

Come here, now. And listen. Our master, the Count of Luna, must find you vigilant. He passes this way to stand near the window of his beloved, where he spends the night hours in watching.

SERVANTS

In his heart fiercely quarrel jealousy's fiery serpents.

FERRANDO

He fears the Trobador*, a valiant rival. Each night he serenades her, just at midnight, beneath her window.

SERVANTS

Heavy sleep overpow'rs us, and must be chased away. Tell us the heart-rending story of Garzia, the brother of our master.

FERRANDO

Gather round, and I will tell the story.

SOLDIERS

May we hear?

SERVANTS *(moving closer)*

Be quiet. Just listen.
(They all surround Ferrando.)

FERRANDO

Our old master, the former Count of Luna,
Blest by Heaven with two lively sons;

Night after night the faithful nurse kept watch,
Guarding the door of the child's room.
Then at break of day on one dire morning
She woke, and with horror she saw . . .
Can you think what she saw beside the infant?

CHORUS

What? What was it? Speak, what was it?

FERRANDO

There stood a gipsy hag, fearsomely glaring,
Clad in a curious garb, witchcraft declaring.
Then on this infant, sleeping in innocence.
She fixed her dark eyes, glistening with virulence.
Shrieking loud, screaming in terror of this fierce one;
Running here, racing there, in search of protection,
The nurse now ran faster than tongue can say 'help me.'
The servants run and come to help her quickly:
They with loud howling seized the bold witch then;
With blows and crying they sent her flying back to her foul den.

CHORUS

And they were right, to show such wrath there,
To drive that witch out to her wild lair.

FERRANDO

But she said she was innocently casting
Horoscopes for his future fate.
O liar! Soon the infant's health was wasting
As he sank 'neath the witch's hate.
His face and limbs grew pale, languid were his motions,
And he shivered the whole night.
The next day we spent in helpless lamentations:

1

---

*It was the Provençal *trobador* who, in the eleventh century, began the tradition of poet-warrior-minstrel that spread through the Romance countries and beyond. *Trovatore, trovador, trouvère, troubadour* — of these the last is the form (from the *langue d'oc*) that has become the most familiar in English. However, in my translation I have preferred the form *trobador* for its primacy, sonority, and geographical aptness. **B.S.**

Ammaliato egli era!

(*Il coro inorridisce.*)
La fattucchiera perseguitata,
Fu presa e al rogo fu condannata:
Ma rimanea la maledetta
Figlia, ministra di ria vendetta!
Compi quest' empia nefando eccesso!
Sparve il fanciullo, e si rinvenne
Mal spenta brace, nel sito stesso
Ov'arsa un giorno la strega venne!
E d'un bambino, ohimé, l'ossame
Bruciato a mezzo, fumante ancor!

CORO

Ah, scellerata! Oh, donna infame!
Del par m'investe odio ed orror!
E il padre?

FERRANDO

Brevi e tristi giorni visse; pure ignoto
del cor presentimento gli diceva, che
spento non era il figlio; ed, a morir
vicino, bramò che il signor nostro a
lui giurasse di non cessar le indagini.
Ah! fur vane!

UOMINI D' ARME

E di colei non si ebbe contezza mai?

FERRANDO

Nulla contezza! Oh! dato mi fosse
rintracciarla un dì!

FAMIGLIARI

Ma ravvisarla potresti?

FERRANDO

Calcolando gli anni trascorsi lo potrei.

UOMINI D' ARME

Sarebbe tempo presso la madre all' inferno spedirla.

FERRANDO

All'inferno? E credenza, che dimori ancor nel mondo l'anima perduta dell'-
empia strega, e quando il cielo è nero
in varie forme altrui si mostri.

CORO

È vero!
Sull' orlo dei tetti alcun l'ha veduta!
In upupa o strige talora si muta!
In corvo tal' altra; più spesso in civetta,
Sull'alba fuggente al par di saetta!

FERRANDO

Morì di paura un servo del Conte,
Che avea della zingara percossa la
fronte!

(*Tutti si pingono di superstizioso
terrore.*)

Apparve a costui d' un gufo in sem-
bianza,
Nell'alta quiete di tacita stanza!
Con occhio lucente guardava, guardava,
Il cielo attristando d'un urlo feral!
Allor mezzanotte appunto suonava . . .

(*Una campana suona mezzanotte.*)

TUTTI

Ah! sia maledetta la strega infernal!

(*Gli Uomini d' Arme accorrono in fondo; i Famigliari corrono verso la
porta.*)

SCENA 2

*Giardini del palazzo; sulla destra, mar-
morea scalinata che mette agli appartamenti. La notte è inoltrata; dense
nubi cuoprono la luna.*

INES

Che più t'arresti? L'ora è tarda, vieni.
Di te la regal donna chiese, l' udisti.

LEONORA

Un' altra notte ancora senza vederlo!

The gipsy had bewitched him!

(*The Chorus shudders.*)

Quickly the servants pursued the old one,

Took her and bound her, doomed her to burning.

There was a daughter, more skilled at witchcraft,

Vile as her mother joined with a demon.

Fearfully fulfilled she the curse of her mother:

She stole the boy—we could find of him no traces.

But at the place where the old witch was burned,

The place where we put an end to her wickedness forever,

There we found later . . . Oh, God! . . . some bones half burned away,

And they continued smoking till they burned away.

CHORUS

How could there be so accursed a woman;

My heart is bursting with hate for her!

And the father?

FERRANDO

Some few days he lived thereafter. But a strange thought came to him in those sad last days: he believed that his stolen son was still alive, and with his dying breath made his son, our master, promise that he would still strive to find his missing brother. Ah, but vainly.

SOLDIERS

And what of her? The daughter of the witch you burned?

FERRANDO

Utterly vanished. If I have the fortune, some day I shall find her.

SERVANTS

And do you think you would know her?

FERRANDO

Even after all these years I would know her. Yes, I'd know her!

SOLDIERS

How glad we'd be if we could send her down to Hell to join her mother.

FERRANDO

Down to Hell? It's believed that she still wanders here on earth; restless in her soul still, that wicked sorceress. And when the sky is darkened, in various guises she comes to haunt us.

CHORUS

It's true!

On roofs of high houses they say that they've seen her,

In shape of a screech owl or other grim creature.

Sometimes she will fly as a crow in the evening,

But always she will disappear with the dawning.

FERRANDO

A servant who saw her all gruesome and horrid

Was killed in an instant when she touched his forehead.

He died of his fear when she walked through the halls

In the shape of an owl,

(*They all cringe in superstitious terror.*)

And the room all about was as still as a tomb.

Her eyes glowed like flames to a horrible height,

As the heavens resounded with howl after howl.

Just then the clock slowly struck the hour of midnight.

(*A bell sounds midnight.*)

FERRANDO AND CHORUS

Ah, may God hear us as we send our curse on this infernal witch.

(*The soldiers hasten to their places at the back; the servants run to the door.*)

SCENE II

The gardens of the palace: to the right, marble steps which lead to the apartments. The night is well advanced; thick clouds cover the moon.

INES

Why do you stop here? Come along, please. It's late. The queen will want to speak with you. You know that.

LEONORA

And will another night pass without my seeing him?

INES

Perigliosa fiamma tu nutri! Oh come,
dove la primiera favilla in te s'apprese?

LEONORA

Ne' torneì. V'apparve, bruno le vesti
ed il cimier, lo scudo bruno e di
stemma ignudo, sconosciuto guerrier,
che dell' agone gli onori ottenne—al
vincitor sul crine il serto io posi—
civil guerra intanto arse—nol vidi
più! Come d' aurato sogno, fuggente
imago! ed era volta lunga stagion—
ma poi . . .

INES

Che avvenne?

LEONORA

Ascolta.
Tacea la notte placida
E bella in ciel sereno;
La luna il viso argenteo
Mostrava lieto e pieno!
Quando suonar per l'aere,
Infino allor sì muto,
Dolci s'udiro e flebili
Gli accordi di un liuto,
E versi melanconici,
Un trovator cantò.
Versi di prece ed umile,
Qual d'uom che prega Iddio:
In quella ripeteasi
Un nome, il nome mio!
Corsi al veron sollecita . . .
Egli era, egli era desso!
Gioja provai che agli angeli
Solo è provar concesso!
Al core, al guardo estatico
La terra un ciel sembrò!

INES

Quanto narrasti di turbamento m'ha
piena l' alma!—Io temo . . .

LEONORA

Invano!

INES

Dubbio ma tristo presentimento in me
risveglia quest'uomo arcano!
Tenta obliarlo—

LEONORA

Che dici! Oh basti!

INES

Cedi al consiglio dell'amistà, cedi . . .

LEONORA

Obliarlo! Ah! tu parlasti
Detto, che intendere l' alma non sa.
Di tale amor, che dirsi
Mal può dalla parola,
D'amor, che intendo io sola,
Il cor s'inebriò.
Il mio destino compirsi
Non può che a lui d'appresso.
S'io non vivrò per esso,
Per esso morirò!

INES (*da sè*)

Non debba mai pentirsi
Chi tanto un giorno amò!

(*Ascendono agli appartamenti.*)

CONTE

Tace la notte! Immersa nel sonno è
certo la regal signora; ma veglia la sua
dama! Oh! Leonora! Tu desta sei;
mel dice da quel verone, tremolante
un raggio della notturna lampa. Ah!
l' amorosa fiamma m'arde ogni fibra!
Ch'io ti vegga è d'uopo . . . Che tu
m' intenda, vengo. A noi supremo è
tal momento!

(*Cieco d' amore avviasi verso la gradi-
nata: odonsi gli accordi di un liuto;
egli si arresta.*)

Il trovator! Io fremo!

MANRICO

Deserto sulla terra,
Col rio destino in guerra,
È sola speme un cor,
Un cor al trovator.
Ma s'ei quel cor possiede,
Bello di casta fede,
È d'ogni re maggior,
Il trovator!

CONTE

Oh detti! Oh, gelosia!
Non m' inganno. Ella scende!

(*Si avvolge nel suo mantello.*)

INES

What a dangerous love you are cherishing. O tell me, where did you fall in love with this dark stranger?

LEONORA

At the tournament. He strode out, clad all in black from head to toe; and no one knew him, the boldest man here. That day in the fighting, he conquered each foe who came against him. On his victorious brow I placed the laurel. But when civil war began here, he came no more. Yet through my golden visions floated his image; and then my visions also disappeared. Until . . .

INES

What happened?

LEONORA

I'll tell you!
The air so still, so mild the night,
The sky serene and calmly bright.
The moon sent forth its silvery light
Nowhere was there more heavenly
    sight.
Then came a sound that filled the air,
Air that had been so peaceful.
Ne'er heard I voice so thrilling and
    fair,
Enriched by stroke of lute so full;
In melancholy verses came his song
    that pierced me to the heart:
It was a trobador!
Verses of holy prayer he sang,
As one would pray to God Himself.
And through his song but one name
    rang—
He sang there to Leonora!
I ran to the window breathlessly—
He was there, my only dear one.
Joy filled my heart so rapturously,
More bliss is felt by angels alone.
My heart, my eyes, in ecstasy
Saw earth transformed to heaven,
Heaven seemed but earth to me!

INES

What you have told me fills me with terror. Woe seems to threaten; I warn you.

LEONORA

You must not.

INES

Gloomy foreboding comes with your story. Do you not fear this mysterious stranger? You must forget him.

LEONORA

Forget him? I cannot!

INES

Oh, hear the counsel of one who loves you. Hear me.

LEONORA

I forget him? Now you are pleading vainly, for never can I forget.
Of such a love as I now feel
No words I speak can ever tell.
Such love intoxicates the soul—
The soul is drunk with love that it cannot conceal.
My fate is tied to one I love;
I cannot leave him though I try.
If I am not his bride while I live,
Perhaps I may be his at last when I die.

INES (aside)

I pray that she may not know
What such love bears in woe.
(They ascend to their quarters.)

COUNT

How still the night is. The queen surely sleeps, protected by a lady keeping a faithful, loving watch there. Leonora, now by the glare of the lantern which sends its light down through your window, I know and suffer your sleepless night with you. Ah, how the wound of love's dart runs through all my heart. But now I must see you, and you must hear me—hear me in this most blissful moment when our hearts are one.
(Blinded with love, he makes for the steps. Suddenly he hears the sound of a lute and halts.)
The Trobador! Damnation!

MANRICO

Deserted, no haven anywhere,
His heart has one hope more,
Love still worth living for.
One love and then no more,
Love for the Trobador!
But if that love be his to hold,
Then no one is more bold,
No king has greater power,
If only she would love
Her Trobador!

COUNT

What is this? . . . I rage and shudder.
. . . Am I dreaming? She approaches.
(He wraps himself in his cloak.)

LEONORA

(*correndo verso il Conte*)

Anima mia!

CONTE

(Che far?)

LEONORA

Più dell' usato è tarda l' ora; io ne
contai gl'instanti, coi palpiti del core!
Alfin ti guida pietoso amor tra queste
braccia.

LA VOCE DEL TROVATORE

Infida!

(*La luna mostrasi dai nugoli, e lascia
scorgere una persona, di cui la vi-
siera nasconde il volto.*)

LEONORA

(*riconoscendo entrambi, e gettandosi
ai piedi di Manrico*)

Qual voce! Ah, dalle tenebre
Tratta in errore io fui!
A te credei rivolgere
L' accento, e non a lui . . .
A te, che l'alma mia
Sol chiede, sol desia!
Io t'amo, il giuro, t'amo
D'immenso, eterno amor!

CONTE

Ed osi?

MANRICO (*sollevandola*)

Ah più non bramo!

CONTE

Avvampo di furor!
Se un vil non sei, discovriti!

LEONORA

Ohimè!

CONTE

Palesa il nome!

LEONORA (*piano a Manrico*)

Deh per pietà!

MANRICO

Ravvisami, Manrico io son!

CONTE

Tu! Come? Insano, temerario! D'
Urgel seguace, a morte proscritto,
ardisci volgerti a queste regie porte?

MANRICO

Che tardi? Or via le guardie appella,
ed il rivale al ferro del carnefice
consegna!

CONTE

Il tuo fatale istante assai più prossimo
è, dissenato! Vieni . . .

LEONORA

Conte!

CONTE

Al mio sdegno vittima è forza ch'io ti
sveni!

LEONORA

Oh, ciel! T'arresta!

CONTE

Seguimi!

MANRICO

Andiam!

LEONORA (*a parte*)

Che mai farò? Un sol mio grido perde-
re lo puote! M' odi!

CONTE

No! Di geloso amor sprezzato,
Arde in me tremendo fuoco!
Il tuo sangue, o sciagurato,
Ad estinguerlo fia poco!

(*a Leonora*)

Dirgli, o folle, io t'amo ardisti!
Ei più vivere non può.
Un accento proferisti,
Che a morir lo condannò!

LEONORA

Un istante almen dia loco
Il tuo sdegno alla ragione:
Io, sol io di tanto foco
Son, pur troppo, la cagione!

LEONORA
(*running toward the Count*)
Oh, my beloved . . .

COUNT
(What's this?)

LEONORA
Tonight you are so late I trembled; I
thought you were not coming. But
love took pity on me, and brought
you here where my arms can hold
you warmly, press you to my heart.

THE VOICE OF MANRICO
Ah, false one!
(*The moon emerges from the clouds
and makes visible a person whose
face is hidden by a mask.*)

LEONORA
(*recognizing both men, and throwing
herself at Manrico's feet*)
What voice is that? Ah, in the dark-
ness here
I was betrayed by shadows.
To you I thought my heart spoke clear,
To you alone my love goes.
My soul will leave you never.
Now read this truth in my eyes:
'Tis you I love forever
With love that never dies.

COUNT
Can this be?

MANRICO (*raising her*)
What bliss you bring me.

COUNT
With rage my heart is burning.

LEONORA
I love you.

COUNT
Rage consumes my heart. Unless you
fear, reveal yourself.

LEONORA
Alas.

COUNT
Your name I must know.
LEONORA (*imploringly, to Manrico*)
Oh, please take pity.

MANRICO
Behold me then: Manrico.

COUNT
You? No, no. Insane one. You were
sentenced, condemned to die, con-
victed of treason. Have you become
insane, to come within these portals?

MANRICO
Why stand there? Just call the guards,
give orders. Your only rival stands
here; you can consign him to the
headsman.

COUNT
Your death is closer than you dream,
for I shall be your headsman. Come,
then.

LEONORA
Hear me.

COUNT
You shall fall beneath my sword, the
victim of my vengeance.

LEONORA
Oh God, please stop them!

COUNT
Follow me!

MANRICO
I come!

LEONORA (*aside*)
What shall I do? A single cry from me,
and it may doom him.
Hear me!

COUNT
No. Jealousy has frozen all my feelings.
Rage within me burns with white-hot
fervor.
Blood alone can quench my passion,
Blood from you alone can soothe my
hatred.
(*to Leonora*)
You, Oh mad one, have said that you
love him.
How may I endure his living?
You yourself have said the words that
doom him;
When you confessed your love for him
You sent him to his death for love.

LEONORA
Let your wrath now be tempered with
mercy.
Reason must rule your fearful anger.
I alone led him into this danger;
Trusting, hoping, he comes to win
me—

Piombi il tuo furore
Sulla rea che t'oltraggiò,
Vibra il ferro in questo core,
Che te amar non vuol, nè può!

MANRICO

Del superbo è vana l' ira,
Ei cadrà, da me trafitto;
Il mortal, che amor t'inspira,
Dall' amor fu reso invitto!

(al Conte)

La tua sorte è già compita,
L'ora omai per te suonò!
Il tuo core e la tua vita
Il destino a me serbò!

(I due rivali si allontanano con le spade sguainate. Leonora cade, priva di sentimento.)

ATTO SECONDO

LA GITANA

SCENA 1

Un diruto abituro sulle falde d'un monte della Biscaglia; nel fondo, quasi tutto aperto, arde un gran fuoco. I primi albori.

Azucena siede presso il fuoco, Manrico le sta disteso accanto sopra una coltrice, ed avviluppato nel suo mantello: ha l'elmo ai piedi, e fra le mani la spada, su cui figge immobilmente lo sguardo. Una banda di zingari è sparsa all'intorno.

ZINGARI

Vedi! le fosche notturne spoglie
De'cieli sveste l'immensa volta;
Sembra una vedova che alfin si toglie
I bruni panni ond'era involta.
All' opra! Dagli martella!
Chi del gitano i giorni abbella?
La Zingarella!
Versami un tratto: lena e coraggio
Il corpo e l'anima traggon dal bere.

Oh guarda, guarda! del sole un raggio
Brilla più vivido nel tuo bicchiere!
All'opra, all'opra—dagli martella
Quale a voi splende propizia stella
La Zingarella!

AZUCENA

(Canta; gli zingari le si fanno allato.)
Stride la vampa!

La folla indomita
Corre a quel fuoco
Lieta in sembianza!
Urli di gioia
D'intorno echeggiano:
Cinta di sgherri
Donna s'avanza!
Sinistra splende
Sui volti orribili
La tetra fiamma
Che s'alza al ciel!
Stride la vampa, giunge la vittima
Nero vestita, discinta e scalza!
Grido feroce di morte levasi,
L'eco il ripete di balza in balza!
Sinistra splende sui volti orribili
La tetra fiamma che s'alza al ciel!

ZINGARI

Mesta è la tua canzon!

AZUCENA

Del pari mesta che la storia funesta
da cui tragge argomento!

(Rivolge il capo dalla parte di Manrico, e mormora sommessamente.)

Mi vendica, mi vendica!

MANRICO (a parte)

L'arcana parola ognor!

VECCHIO ZINGARO

Compagni, avanza il giorno; a procacciarci un pan, su su! scendiamo per le propinque villa.

Seeking, dreaming, for my heart within
me.
Vengeance may not on him be in-
flicted;
Let your fury to me be directed.
Not your love but your sword touches
me.

MANRICO

Pride and wrath will avail not to save
him.
His doom will come through this, my
sword:
Through the courage that your love
now gives him
Any man becomes victorious lord.
(to the Count)
Fate now tells you that your days are
ended.
Fate now gives your life into my power.
Ne'er will love be more bravely de-
fended;
Fate smiles on me in this glorious hour.
(The two rivals depart with drawn
swords. Leonora falls, losing con-
sciousness.)

ACT II

THE GIPSY WOMAN

SCENE I

*A ruined abode on the slopes of a
mountain near Biscay; at the back,
in the open, burns a great fire. Nearly
dawn. Azucena is sitting near the
fire; Manrico is lying near her on a
pallet; he is wrapped in his cloak,
his helmet is at his feet. In his hands
is a sword, which he gazes at intently.
A band of gipsies is scattered about.*

GIPSIES

See how the clouds melt away from the
face of the sky
When the sun shines, its brightness
beaming;
Just as a widow, discarding her black
robes,
Shows all her beauty in brilliance
gleaming . . .
And so to work now. Lift up your
hammers!
Who turns the gipsy's day from gloom
to brightest sunshine?
His lovely gipsy maid!
Fill up the goblets! New strength and
courage

Flow from lusty wine to soul and body.
Look now and see where the rays of
the sun
Play and sparkle and give to our wine
gay new splendor . . .
And so to work now.
Who turns the gipsy's day from gloom
to brightest sunshine?
His lovely gipsy maid!

AZUCENA

(*She sings; the gipsies gather round
her.*)
Wild flames are soaring,
Crowds fiercely roaring.
Madly they rush about,
Ready God Himself to flout.
Howlings of gruesome glee
Echo through the valley.
Brutal soldiers in their ire
Drag a woman to the fire.
Slowly the fire wanes,
Drinking blood from her veins.
Flames multiply, mounting on high—
They soar to the sky . . .
Fiercely the flames roar,
Now casting fear into all.
The poor victim all in black,
Quivers in terror.
Shrieks ring exultantly,
Echoing to and fro.
Hills hear the victim's cries,
Give back the echo.
Fearsome is the leaping flame,
Shining on the faces about.
Blood-lusting fire, greedy fire,
Which soars to the sky.

GIPSIES

Sad is the song you sing.

AZUCENA

Far sadder are the thoughts which
come to me when I recall the death
of that poor woman. (*turning her
head towards Manrico and murmur-
ing softly*) "Avenge my death!"

MANRICO (*aside*)

Once more these mysterious words.

AN OLD GIPSY

The day is here, companions, the day's
work lies ahead. So now be off to the
town that lies below us.

ZINGARI

Andiamo.

(*Tutti scendono alla rinfusa giù per la china: tratto tratto e sempre a maggior distanza, odesi il loro canto.*)

Chi del gitano i giorni abbella?
La Zingarella!

MANRICO (*sorgendo*)

Soli or siamo! Deh, narra quella storia funesta.

AZUCENA

E tu la ignori, tu pur? Ma giovinetto, i passi tuoi d'ambizion lo sprone lungi traea! Dell'ava il fine acerbo è quest'istoria. La incolpò superbo conte di malefizio, onde asseria, côlto un bambin suo figlio. Essa bruciata venne dov'arde or quel foco!

MANRICO

(*rifuggendo con raccapriccio dalla fiamma*)

Ahi! Sciagurata!

AZUCENA

Condotta ell'era in ceppi al suo destin tremendo;
Col figlio sulle braccia, io la seguia piangendo.
Infino ad essa un varco tentai, ma invano, aprirmi,
Invan tentò la misera fermarsi e benedirmi!
Chè, fra bestemmie oscene, pungendola coi ferri
Al rogo la cacciavano gli scellerati sgherri!
Allor, con tronco accento; "mi vendica!" sclamò.
Quel detto un'eco eterno in questo cor lasciò.

MANRICO

La vendicasti?

AZUCENA

Il figlio giunsi a rapir del Conte;
Lo trascinai qui meco le fiamme ardean già pronte.

MANRICO

Le fiamme? Oh ciel! Tu forse?

AZUCENA

Ei distruggeasi in pianto
Io mi sentivo il core dilaniato, infranto!
Quand'ecco agl' egri spirti, come in un sogno, apparve
La vision ferale di spaventose larve!
Gli sgherri ed il supplizio! La madre smorta in volto—
Scalza, discinta! il grido, il noto grido ascolto!
"Mi vendica!" La mano convulsa stendo, stringo
La vittima—nel foco la traggo, la sospingo!
Cessa il fatal delirio, l'orrida scena fugge,
La fiamma sol divampa, a la sua preda strugge!
Pur volgo intorno il guardo e innanzi a me vegg'io
Dell'empio Conte il figlio!

MANRICO

Ah! che dici?

AZUCENA

Il figlio mio, mio figlio avea bruciato!

MANRICO

Oh! Quale orror!

AZUCENA

Sul capo mio le chiome sento drizzarsi ancor!

(*Azucena ricade trambasciata sul proprio seggio; Manrico ammutolisce, colpito d'orrore e di sorpresa.*)

MANRICO

Non son tuo figlio?
E chi son io, chi dunque?

AZUCENA

Tu sei mio figlio!

MANRICO

Eppur dicesti . . .

AZUCENA

Ah! forse? Che vuoi! Quando al pensier s'affaccia il truce caso, lo spirto intenebrato pone stolte parole sul mio labbro. Madre, tenera madre non m'avesti ognora?

GIPSIES

Be off, then.

(*They wander off down the slope—their song diminishing with distance.*)

Who turns the gipsy's day from gloom
to brightest sunshine?
His lovely gipsy maid!

MANRICO (*arising*)

No one's with us. Explain this gloomy
story to me now.

AZUCENA

And do you not know it yet? Yes, you
were young then, when ambition
took you from me. How could you
know it? I sang the death of one
whose death breeds evil. Proud in-
deed the noble lord who accused my
mother; she was a witch, he said;
she had his son enchanted. So came
that evil sentence; for this leaped
that fire!

MANRICO

Ah, that was dreadful!

(*recoiling with a shudder from the
flames*)

AZUCENA

In chains, in shameful chains they
bound her;
They dragged her on a path of doom.
I pressed my child to my bosom;
Weeping I came behind her.
I tried to come close to touch her,
Before doom upon her fell.
But vain was all her reaching
Out to kiss me in a last farewell.
Wildly did the crowd revile her;
They shrieked like a mob of madmen!
And with a hellish lust for blood,
They tied her to the stake then.
She called for Death to take her:
"Avenge my death," she cried.
Her words burn in my heart forever,
Words she spoke—and died.

MANRICO

Did you avenge her?

AZUCENA

It came to me, the Count's young son
to kidnap—that he might serve my
vengeance. The flames were still
burning.

MANRICO

The flames? Oh, God! You could not.

AZUCENA

I took the child softly weeping.
His tears were tearing at my heart, as
though he would destroy me.
But quickly there rose before me . . .
just as a dream arises,
That last brutal vision, of one in help-
less weeping.
I hear her hopelessly praying, the pale-
ness of death upon her,
Quivering and quaking. Her outcry,
her hopeless outcry . . .
I hear her: "Avenge my death." I
reach out my hand, imploring,
And touch the child I hold, the flames
leap before me.
I hurl the infant! My fatal madness
leaves me,
Sights of grim horror vanish.
The flames still leap and cackle while
their poor victim struggles.
I look about me wildly, and there I
see . . . beside me . . .
The son of the Count . . . still living!

MANRICO

What? What say you?

AZUCENA

But it was my son, my only child that
I burned.

MANRICO

Oh, what horror! Oh, what woe, what
dreadful woe!

AZUCENA

My guilty head still bears the pain,
My mother's heart still cries in vain.

(*Azucena falls back exhausted on her
seat. Manrico is struck dumb with
horror and surprise.*)

MANRICO

Am I not your son? Then whose son
am I? Who am I?

AZUCENA

You are my true son!

MANRICO

But now, you just said . . .

AZUCENA

What said I? I know not. Whene'er
I think on that dreadful scene of
burning, my mind is whirled about so
that I no longer know what I am
saying. Mother? Tell me, have I not
been a loving mother?

MANRICO

Potrei negarlo?

AZUCENA

A me, se vivi ancora, nol dêi?—Notturna, nei pugnati campi di Pelilla, ove spento fama ti disse, a darti sepoltura non mossi? La fuggente aura vital non iscovrì nel seno, non t'arrestò materno affetto? E quante cure non spesi a risanar le tante ferite!

MANRICO (con nobile orgoglio)

Che portai quel di fatale, ma tutte qui, nel petto! Io sol, fra mille già sbandati, al nemico volgendo ancor la faccia! Il rio Di Luna su me piombò col suo drappello: io caddi, però da forte io caddi!

AZUCENA

Ecco mercede ai giorni, che l'infame nel singolar certame ebbe salva da te! Qual t'acciecava strana pietà per esso?

MANRICO

Oh, madre, non saprei dirlo a me
stesso!
Mal reggendo all'aspro assalto,
Ei già tocco il suolo avea:
Balenava il colpo in alto
Che trafiggerlo dovea
Quando arresta un moto arcano
Nel discender questa mano,
Le mie fibre acuto gelo
Fa repente abbrividir!
Mentre un grido vien dal cielo
Che mi dice: non ferir.

AZUCENA

Ma nell'alma dell'ingrato
Non parlò del cielo il detto!
Oh! se ancor ti spinge il fato
A pugnar col maledetto,
Compi, o figlio, qual d'un Dio,
Compi allor il cenno mio!
Sino all'elsa questa lama
Vibra, immergi all'empio in cor!

(Odesi un prolungato suono di corno.)

MANRICO

L'usato messo Ruiz invia, Forse.

(Dà fiato anch'esso al suo corno.)

AZUCENA

"Mi vendica!"

(Resta concentrata quasi inconsapevole
di ciò che succede.)

Entra il Messo

MANRICO (al messo)

Inoltra il piè.
Guerresco evento, dimmi, seguia?

MESSO

Risponda il foglio che reco a te.

(porgendo il foglio, che Manrico leg-
ge)

MANRICO

"In nostra possa è Castellor; ne deî tu,
per cenno del Prence, vigilar le di-
fese. Ove ti è dato, affrettati a venir.
Giunta la sera, tratta in inganno di
tua morte al grido, nel vicin chiostro
della Croce il velo cingerà Leonora."
(con dolorosa esclamazione) Oh,
giusto cielo!

AZUCENA (scuotendosi)

Che fia?

MANRICO (al messo)

Veloce scendi la balza, ed un cavallo
a me provvedi.

MESSO

Corro.

MANRICO

Could I deny it?

AZUCENA

It is through me that you are still living. When word was brought to me that you had died in battle, was it not I, in darkest midnight, who searched among the dead to find your body? All night long I searched with no one by my side. My eyes failed, it was my mother's heart that found you. And then my tears flowed so freely that to your wounds my tears brought quick healing.

MANRICO

(with lofty pride)

Wounds that brought me only glory; I suffered each one bravely. And only I stood firm on that day, while my comrades dispersed and fled like cowards. That vile di Luna then rushed on me with all his soldiers. I fell then, but fell as does a hero!

AZUCENA

This was his thanks for the life that you had spared him, although his life was forfeit when he lost in single combat. Why did you show mercy? Mercy that blinded reason.

MANRICO

Ah, mother, I cannot tell how it happened.
Long were we fighting; my sword was victorious.
He fell to earth there, his portion was inglorious.
I stood above him, my arm was raised for killing.
Heaven spoke and I must listen, though most unwilling.
Hidden from me was my reason for refraining;
Showing this man mercy was beyond explaining.
I was struck by an icy chill
That made my arm fall to my side:
Sweet came the voices calling down from Heaven,
Speaking to my heart from Heaven,
Softly saying: Kill him not.

AZUCENA

But for such a graceless villain
Never can be heard the voice of angels calling down from Heaven.
If it happens once again
That you should meet this cursed scoundrel,
Fighting him in single combat, hear your mother.
Heed my counsel! Take it to your heart
As it were God's word: Show him no remorse,
But plunge your shining sword into his heart.

(A prolonged sound of a horn is heard.)

MANRICO

There is the call now, perhaps from Ruiz. I'll answer.

(He returns the signal on his horn.)

AZUCENA

"Avenge my death!"

(She remains preoccupied and as though unaware of what follows.)

(The messenger enters.)

MANRICO (to the messenger)

Come here to me. What news do you bring? How goes the battle?

MESSENGER

I have a message that will tell you all.

(He produces a letter, which Manrico reads.)

MANRICO

"The town of Castellor is ours. At the order of the prince you are chosen to defend it. Be brave now, do not falter in your task. Deceived by rumor into thinking you were dead, Leonora has planned, this very night, to take the veil in a nearby convent."

(with an anguished exclamation)

Oh, may God help me!

AZUCENA (coming to herself)

What is this?

MANRICO (to the messenger)

Now quickly, go to the village and have a horse made ready for me.

MESSENGER

Yes, sir.

AZUCENA (*frapponendosi*)

Manrico!

MANRICO

Il tempo incalza! Vola, m'aspetta del
colle ai piedi.

(*Il messo parte, frettolosamente.*)

AZUCENA

E speri e vuoi?

MANRICO (*a parte*)

Perderla! Oh ambascia! Perder quell'
angel!

AZUCENA (*a parte*)

È fuor di se!

MANRICO

Addio!

(*postosi l'elmo sul capo ed afferrando
il mantello*)

AZUCENA

No, ferma, odi!

MANRICO

Mi lascia!

AZUCENA (*autorevole*)

Ferma! Son io che parlo a te!
Perigliarti ancor languente
Per cammin selvaggio ed ermo!
Le ferite vuoi, demente!
Riaprir del petto infermo!
No, soffrirlo non poss'io,
Il tuo sangue è sangue mio!
Ogni stilla che ne versi
Tu la spremi dal mio cor!

MANRICO

Un momento può involarmi
Il mio ben, la mia speranza!
No, che basti ad arrestarmi,
Terra e ciel non han possanza!
Ah, mi sgombra, o madre, i passi,
Guai per te, s'io qui restassi!
Tu vedresti ai piedi tuoi
Spento il figlio di dolor!

AZUCENA

No, soffrirlo non poss'io.

MANRICO

Guai per te, s'io qui restassi!

AZUCENA

No, soffrirlo non poss'io,
Il tuo sangue è sangue mio!

MANRICO

Tu vedresti ai piedi tuoi
Spento il figlio di dolor!

(*Si allontana, indarno trattenuto da
Azucena.*)

SCENA 2

*Chiostro d'un cenobio in vicinanza di
Castellor.—È notte.*

*Il Conte, Ferrando, ed alcuni seguaci,
avviluppati nei lori mantelli, inol-
trandosi cautamente.*

CONTE

Tutto è deserto; nè per l'aura ancora
suona l'usato carme. In tempo io
giungo!

FERRANDO

Ardita opra, o signore, imprendi.

CONTE

Ardita, e quel furente amore ed irritato
orgoglio chiesero a me. Spento il
rival, caduto ogni ostacol sembrava
a' miei desire; novello e più possente
ella ne appresta. L'altare! Ah no!
non fia d'altri Leonora! Leonora è
mia!

Il balen del suo sorriso
D'una stella vince il raggio!
Il fulgor del suo bel viso
Nuovo infonde a me coraggio.
Ah, l'amor, l'amore ond'ardo
Le favelli in mio favor!
Sperda il sole d'un suo sguardo
La tempesta del mio cor.

(*Odesi il rintocco de' sacri bronzi.*)

Qual suono! Oh, ciel!

FERRANDO

La squilla vicino il rito annunzia.

AZUCENA (*intervening*)

Manrico!

MANRICO

No, I must hurry. Go now. Make ready. Await me below there. (*The messenger hastily departs.*)

AZUCENA

What are you now planning?

MANRICO (*aside*)

Am I now to lose her? Lose my dear angel?

AZUCENA (*aside*)

He's lost his mind.

MANRICO

I must go.

(*He puts on his helmet and wraps his cloak about him.*)

AZUCENA

No, stay here. Listen.

MANRICO

I must go.

AZUCENA (*firmly*)

Stay here. Your mother pleads with you.
Do not go on such a dangerous ride,
With your hand unable to hold the rein;
While the blood still flows from your wounded side,
And your face is pallid and racked with pain.
No, I beg you to recall
That when from me you now depart,
Each drop of blood you lightly let fall
Flows as though from my own heart.

MANRICO

I must ride with all speed to my loved one.
To delay at this moment of danger
Is to feel her anguish and pain
No more than if she were but a stranger.
Do not try with your tears now to hold me,
But remember the love that you've told me.
I shall die unless she becomes my wife;
For her love I'll yield my life.

AZUCENA

But I cannot let you go from me.

MANRICO

It is woe for you if I stay behind.

AZUCENA

But I cannot let you go from me.
It is my blood that flows in your veins.

MANRICO

I shall die unless she becomes my wife;
For her I yield my life.

(*Manrico departs, while Azucena tries to hold him back.*)

SCENE II

Cloister of a convent near Castellor. It is night.

The Count, Ferrando, and several followers cautiously enter, wrapped in their cloaks.

COUNT

All now is quiet. The familiar sounds of chanting have died away. I've come in good time.

FERRANDO

A desperate labor surely lies before us.

COUNT

What say you? Can you speak so when love itself and wounded pride command and force me to act? My rival dead, I thought every obstacle conquered, my desires accomplished. But now another threat is here to take her from me: the convent. Ah, no. Not the convent for Leonora. Mine is Leonora.
Her bright smile like lightning flashes,
Sparkles like the starlight, brighter than the sunshine.
And the glory of her eyes would make dead ashes
Rise in glowing splendor—glory
That must be mine.
All my love had frozen in my heart;
Life itself was ready to depart.
Then her face with passion fired me,
And a tempest seized me, and with love inspired me.
All my love and all my yearning
Go to her and seek returning.

(*The tolling of convent bells is heard.*)

That fatal bell! Oh God!

FERRANDO

The bell tolls for a holy procession.

CONTE

Ah! pria che giunga all'altar, si
rapisca!

FERRANDO

Oh, bada!

CONTE

Taci! Non odo! Andate. Di quei faggi
all'ombra celatevi!

(*Ferrando ed i seguaci si allontanano.*)

Ah! fra poco mia diverrà!
Tutto m'investe un foco!

(*Ansioso guardingo osserva dalla parte
onde deve giungere Leonora.*)

FERRANDO E SEGUACI (*sotto voce*)

Ardire! Andiam, celiamoci
Fra l'ombre, nel mister.
Ardire! Andiam, silenzio!
Si compia il suo voler!

CONTE

Per me ora fatale,
I tuoi momenti affretta:
La gioja che m'aspetta,
Gioja mortal non è!
Invanno un Dio rivale
S'oppone all' amor mio,
Non può nemmen un Dio,
Donna, rapirti a me!

(*Raggiunge i suoi nell'interno.*)

CORO INTERNO DI RELIGIOSE

Ah! se l'error t'ingombra,
Oh, figlia d'Eva, i rai,
Presso a morir, vedrai
Che un'ombra, un sogno fu;
Anzi del sogno un'ombra
La speme di quaggiù!
Vieni, e t'asconda il velo
Ad ogni sguardo umano;
Aura, o pensier mondano
Qui vivo più non è!
Al ciel ti volgi, e il cielo
Si schiuderà per te!

(*Entra Leonora, Ines, ed un seguito
muliebre.*)

LEONORA

Perchè piangete?

INES

Ah! dunque tu per sempre ne lasci!

LEONORA

Oh dolci amiche, un riso, una speranza,
un fior la terra non ha per me! Deg-
g'io volgermi a Quel che degli afflitti

è solo sostegno, e dopo i penitenti
giorni, può fra gli eletti al mio perduto bene ricongiungermi un dì. Ter-
gete i rai, e guidatemi all'ara.

CONTE (*irrompendo ad un tratto*)

No! giammai!

DONNE

Il Conte!

LEONORA

Giusto ciel!

CONTE

Per te non havvi che l'ara d'imeneo.

DONNE

Cotanto ardia!

LEONORA

Insano! E qui venisti?

CONTE

A farti mia.

(*Comparisce Manrico.*)

LEONORA

È deggio e posso crederlo?
Ti veggo a me d'accanto!
È questo un sogno, un'estasi,
Un sovrumano incanto!
Non regge a tanto giubilo
Rapito il cor, sorpreso!
Sei tu dal ciel disceso,
O in ciel son io con te?

CONTE

Dunque gli estinti lasciano
Di morte il regno eterno!
A danno mio rinunzia
Le prede sue l'inferno!
Ma se non mai si fransero
De' giorni tuoi gli stami,
Se vivi e viver brami,
Fuggi da lei, da me.

MANRICO

Nè m'ebbe il ciel, nè l'orrido
Varco infernal sentiero.
Infami sgherri vibrano
Mortali colpi, è vero!

COUNT

Before she reaches the altar we must seize her.

FERRANDO

Be careful.

COUNT

Silence. I fear not. Come hither. In the shade of those trees we shall hide ourselves.

Leonora, soon you are mine! The fire of my love is burning.

(*Ferrando and the followers withdraw.*)

(*The Count anxiously and watchfully looks in the direction from which Leonora will come.*)

FERRANDO AND CHORUS

(*in an undertone*)

Be bold, but come conceal yourselves
Behind those trees. We must be still.
We must obey his will.

COUNT

To me now speaks a voice divine
And I await the answer to my prayer.
The hope that she will soon be mine
Is joy much more than mortal heart can bear.
In vain might God Himself now try to halt my plan
To make Leonora mine forever.

(*withdraws to the background*)

CHORUS OF NUNS (*within*)

Ah, if the chains of error,
Daughter of Eve, have bound you,
Know when you come to Death's door,
God offers you His grace.
And when life's dream is over
You'll see Him face to face.
Come then and let this veil
Shroud you from earthly eyes,
Free you from earth's dark jail,
Win for you Heaven's prize.
Walk evermore by God's side;
He'll take you as His bride.

(*Leonora, Ines and companions enter.*)

LEONORA

But why are you weeping?

INES

For ever, you will leave me for ever.

LEONORA

My dear companion, the gladness, the joy that earth has . . . the hopes, above all, no more for me. To God alone can I turn, to whom the afflicted one goes for solace. And after years of penitential prayers I may be united with my lover, nevermore to part. So dry your tears; lead me now to the altar.

COUNT (*enters suddenly*)

No, you will not.

INES AND COMPANIONS

The Count!

LEONORA

Oh, dear heaven!

COUNT

For you no altar but that of lawful marriage.

INES AND COMPANIONS

What burning passion!

LEONORA

O mad one, why are you here?

COUNT

To make you my bride.

(*Manrico appears.*)

LEONORA

Can I in truth believe my eyes?
Are you now standing before me?
What sort of vision or fantasy,
What magic, what wondrous enchantment?
I cannot believe what my own eyes tell me;
My heart cannot hold such joy.
Have you come down from Heaven,
Or am I raised to you?

COUNT

Can then the dead escape
The eternal regions of the underworld?
Does Hell renounce its claim
Only to annoy and vex me?
Still the thread of life is in you;
The thread of life has not been cut.
Yet if you still live and still hope to live
You must now flee—flee from her and flee from me.

MANRICO

Hell has not seized me,
Nor have I yet been claimed by Heaven.
Your wicked villains fell on me
And left me sorely wounded.
Power too strong for you to resist—

Potenza irresistibile
Hanno de' fiumi l'onde;
Ma gli empi un Dio confonde!
Quel Dio soccorse a me!

DONNE (*a Leonora*)

Il cielo in cui fidasti,
Pietade avea di te.

FERRANDO E SEGUACI (*al Conte*)

Tu col destin contrasti,
Suo difensore egli è.

(*Entra Ruiz, seguito da armati.*)

RUIZ E ARMATI

Urgel viva!

MANRICO

Miei prodi guerrieri!

RUIZ

Vieni!

MANRICO (*a Leonora*)

Donna, mi segui.

CONTE (*opponendosi*)

E tu speri?

LEONORA

Ah!

MANRICO (*al Conte*)

T'arresta!

CONTE (*sguainando la spada*)

Involarmi costei! No!

RUIZ E ARMATI (*accerchiando il Conte*)

Vaneggia!

FERRANDO E SEGUACI

Che tenti, signor?
(*Il Conte è disarmato da quei di Ruiz.*)

CONTE

(*con gesti ed accenti di maniaco furore*)
Di ragione ogni lume perdei!

LEONORA

M'atterrisce!

MANRICO

Fia supplizio la vita per te!

CONTE

Ho le furie nel cor!

RUIZ E ARMATI (*a Manrico*)

Vieni, è lieta la sorte per te.

FERRANDO E SEGUACI (*al Conte*)

Cedi; or ceder viltade non è!
(*Manrico tragge seco Leonora. Il Conte è respinto, le donne rifuggono al cenobio. Scende subito la tela.*)

ATTO TERZO

IL FIGLIO DELLA ZINGARA

SCENA 1

Accampamento. A destra padiglione del Conte di Luna, su cui sventola la bandiera in segno di supremo comando. Da lungi torreggia Castellor. Entra Ferrando, dal padiglione del Conte.

UOMINI D'ARME

Or co' dadi, ma fra poco
Giuocherem ben altro giuoco!
Questo acciar, dal sangue or terso,
Fia di sangue in breve asperso!

(*Odonsi strumenti guerreschi: tutti si volgono là dove si avanza il suono.*)

Il soccorso dimandato!

(*Un grosso drappello di Balestrieri, traversa il campo.*)

Han l'aspetto del valor!
Più l'assalto ritardato
Or non fia di Castellor.

FERRANDO

Sì, prodi amici; al dì novello, è mente del capitan la rocca investir d'ogni parte. Colà pingue bottino certezza è rinvenir, più che speranza. Si vinca; è nostro.

UOMINI D'ARME

Tu c'inviti a **danza**!

As are the waves of ocean,
So is this God who confounds the
  wicked:
It is this God who has saved me.

INES AND COMPANIONS
(to Leonora)
It's Heaven that has sent him here;
Your trust in Heaven has been
  answered.

FERRANDO AND FOLLOWERS
(to the Count)
You fight in vain, for Fate has always
  rescued him;
In vain do you oppose him.
(Enter Ruiz, followed by soldiers.)

RUIZ AND SOLDIERS
Long live Manrico!

MANRICO
Ah, welcome my comrades.

RUIZ
Come now.

MANRICO *(to Leonora)*
Come now, my lady.

COUNT *(opposing him)*
Dare you hope this?

LEONORA
Ah.

MANRICO *(to the Count)*
Hold back, there.

COUNT *(brandishing his sword)*
You'll not take her from me. No.

RUIZ AND SOLDIERS
(surrounding the Count)
What madness!

FERRANDO AND FOLLOWERS
What would you, my lord?
(The Count is disarmed by Ruiz' men.)

COUNT
*(with the gestures and tones of mad
  fury)*
This is madness that comes now on
  me.

LEONORA
I feel terror.

MANRICO
Kneel now and pray that your life
  may be spared.

COUNT
Madness rages in me.

RUIZ AND SOLDIERS
(to Manrico)
Come now, for Fate favors you.

FERRANDO AND FOLLOWERS
(to the Count)
Yield now; to yield brings no shame.
*(Manrico goes off with Leonora. The
Count is driven back; the women re-
turn to the convent. The curtain
falls fast.)*

ACT III

THE SON OF THE GYPSY
WOMAN

SCENE I

*An encampment. To the right, the
pavilion of the Count of Luna; from
it flies the insignia of a supreme
commander. In the distance, the
towers of the fortress of Castellor.
Ferrando enters from the Count's
tent.*

CHORUS OF SOLDIERS
Now we gamble but soon we play
Games of fighting in which we all pay.
And our swords so whitely gleaming
Will blaze red with blood all streaming.
*(The clash of arms is heard; all turn
  in the direction of the sound.)*
Here come those we have awaited . . .
*(A large group of bowmen cross the
  field in full regalia.)*
And they have a look of strength.
Now we must delay no longer
To assault our ancient foe at Castellor.

FERRANDO
My brave companions. At break of
  daylight our noble captain has re-
  solved to storm that castle and to
  take it. We hope to find great booty
  there. Nay, we're sure to find far
  more than you dream of. If we
  triumph, it is all yours!

SOLDIERS
Triumph or we die there.

FERRANDO E IL CORO

Squilli, echeggi la tromba guerriera,
Chiami all'armi, alla pugna, all'assalto,
Fia domani la nostra bandiera
Di quei merli piantata sull'alto.
No, giammai non sorrise vittoria
Di più liete speranze finor!
Ivi l'util ci aspetta e la gloria,
Ivi opimi la preda e l'onor!

(*Entra il Conte, uscito dalla tenda, e volge uno sguardo bieco a Castellor.*)

CONTE

In braccio al mio rival! Questo pensiero come persecutor demone, ovunque m'insegue. In braccio al mio rival! Ma corro, surta appena l'aurora, io corro a separarvi.—Oh, Leonora!

(*Odonsi tumulti. Entra Ferrando.*)

Che fu?

FERRANDO

D'appresso al campo s'aggirava una zingara: sorpresa da' nostri esploratori, si volse in fuga; essi, a ragion temendo una spia nella trista, l'inseguir.

CONTE

Fu raggiunta?

FERRANDO

È presa.

CONTE

Vista l'hai tu?

FERRANDO

No. Della scorta il condottier m'apprese l'evento.

(*tumulto più vicino*)

Eccola!

(*Azucena con le mani legate, è trascinata dagli esploratori. Un codazzo d'altri soldati.*)

ESPLORATORI

Innanzi, o strega, innanzi!

AZUCENA

Aita! Mi lasciate! Ah, furibondi!
Che mal fec'io?

CONTE

S'appressi.

(*Azucena è tratta innanzi al Conte.*)

A me rispondi, e tremi dal mentir!

AZUCENA

Chiedi.

CONTE

Ove vai?

AZUCENA

Nol so.

CONTE

Che?

AZUCENA

D'una zingara è costume muover senza disegna il passo vagabondo, ed è suo tetto il ciel, sua patria il mondo.

CONTE

E vieni?

AZUCENA

Da Biscaglia, ove finora le sterili montagne ebbia ricetto.

CONTE (*a parte*)

Da Biscaglia!

FERRANDO (*a parte*)

Che intesi! Oh, qual sospetto!

AZUCENA

Giorni poveri vivea,
Pur contenta del mio stato,
Sola speme un figlio avea—
Mi lasciò!—m'oblia, l'ingrato!
Io, deserta, vado errando
Di quel figlio ricercando,
Di quel figlio che al mio core
Pene orribili costò!
Qual per esso provo amore
Madre in terra non provò!

FERRANDO (*a parte*)

Il suo volto!

CONTE

Di', traesti lunga etade fra quei monti?

FERRANDO AND CHORUS

Hear how the trumpet is calling us to battle,
And our hearts are stirred to hear its martial blaring.
Swords are agleam while our sabers loudly rattle,
And our eyes with hatred for the foe are glaring.
Never shall we halt till the castle is our prize;
Behold the conquered foe aghast before our might.
Fame for a soldier such a triumph glorifies
And leaves his name ablaze with splendid light.

(*The Count comes out of his tent and directs a threatening look at Castellor.*)

COUNT

She's in my rival's arms! This thought pursues me like a persecuting demon, and keeps me from resting. Leonora in his arms! But courage! With the first beams of morning she shall be his no longer. Oh, Leonora!

(*Great noise. Ferrando enters.*)

What's that?

FERRANDO

Outside the camp a gipsy woman was seen hovering. When she was challenged by our sentries, she tried to escape them. They had good reason to suspect her as a cursed spy then. They followed her.

COUNT

Was she captured?

FERRANDO

They took her.

COUNT

Have you seen her?

FERRANDO

No, but the captain of the guard informed me about her.
There she is!

(*a noise nearby*)

(*Azucena, her hands bound, is dragged in by the patrol; a group of other soldiers follows.*)

GUARDS

You evil gipsy, come forward!

AZUCENA

Oh, help me. Let me be now. Ah, you are madmen. What harm have I done?

COUNT

Come closer.

(*Azucena is dragged toward the Count.*)

Now give me answer, and see you do not lie.

AZUCENA

Ask me.

COUNT

Where were you going?

AZUCENA

Who knows?

COUNT

What?

AZUCENA

It is the way of the gipsies, without plan to wander. They go about like pilgrims, their only roof the sky, their homeland the wide world.

COUNT

Whence come you?

AZUCENA

Out of Biscay, where until lately I made my lonely home amid savage mountains.

COUNT (*aside*)

Out of Biscay?

FERRANDO (*aside*)

What says she? Oh, what I fear now!

AZUCENA

There I lived in barren poverty,
But contented with my fate.
My one son was deep joy to me,
Till he left me—that ingrate.
And so I, weary and lonely,
Wander, my story to relate
Of that son who makes me go sadly
And for whom I ever wait.
Oh, what mother has such heartbreak,
Despairing for a child's selfish sake.

FERRANDO (*aside*)

Oh, those features!

COUNT

Speak, how long have you lived there, amidst the mountains?

AZUCENA

Lunga, sì.

CONTE

Rammenteresti un fanciul, prole di Conti, involato al suo castello, son tre lustri, e tratto quivi?

AZUCENA

E tu—parla—sei?

CONTE

Fratello del rapito.

AZUCENA (*a parte*)

Ah!

FERRANDO

(*a parte, notando il mal nascosto terrore di Azucena*)

Sì!

CONTE

Ne udivi mai novella?

AZUCENA

Io? No! Concedi che del figlio l'orme io scopra.

FERRANDO

Resta, iniqua!

AZUCENA

Ohimè!

FERRANDO

Tu vedi chi l'infame, orribil opra commettea!

CONTE

Finisci.

FERRANDO

È dessa!

AZUCENA (*piano a Ferrando*)

Taci.

FERRANDO

È dessa che il bambino arse!

CONTE

Ah, perfida!

CORO

Ella stessa!

AZUCENA

Ei mentisce!

CONTE

Al tuo destino or non fuggi.

AZUCENA

Deh!

CONTE

Quei nodi più stringete.

(*I soldati eseguiscono.*)

AZUCENA

Oh, Dio! Oh, Dio!

CORO

Urla pur!

AZUCENA

E tu non vieni, oh, Manrico, oh, figlio mio?

Non soccorri all'infelice madre tua?

CONTE

Di Manrico genitrice!

FERRANDO

Trema!

CONTE

Oh sorte, in mio poter!

AZUCENA

Deh, rallentate, o barbari,
Le acerbe mie ritorte—
Questo crudel martirio
È prolungata morte!
D'iniquo genitore
Empio figliuol peggiore,
Trema, v'è Dio pei miseri,
E Dio ti punirà.

CONTE

Tua prole, o turpe zingara,
Colui, quel traditore?
Potrò col tuo supplizio
Ferirlo in mezzo al core!
Gioja m'inonda il petto,
Cui non esprime il detto!
Meco il fraterno cenere
Piena vendetta avrà!

FERRANDO E CORO

Infame pira sorgere,
Vedrai, vedrai tra poco,
Nè solo tuo supplizio
Sarà terreno foco!
Le vampe dell'inferno
A te fian rogo eterno!
Ivi penare ed ardere
L'ànima tua dovrà!

(*Al cenno del Conte, i soldati traggono seco loro Azucena. Egli entra nella tenda, seguito da Ferrando.*)

AZUCENA

Long, my lord.

COUNT

Do you remember that a child, son of
the Count, was basely stolen from his
castle, twenty years since, and never
seen more?

AZUCENA

And you . . . are you that son?

COUNT

No, no, I am his brother.

AZUCENA (aside)

Ah . . .

FERRANDO (aside)

Yes!

COUNT

(noticing the ill-concealed terror of
Azucena)

Do you know aught about him?

AZUCENA

Do I? No. Release me now that I may
seek my son.

FERRANDO

Stay, thou base one!

AZUCENA

Alas.

FERRANDO

Here is that cruel one who did that
monstrous deed of evil.

COUNT

Can this be?

FERRANDO

This is she.

AZUCENA (softly to Ferrando)

Silence.

FERRANDO

This is the wicked one who burned the
infant.

COUNT

Ah, murderess.

CHORUS

We have found her!

AZUCENA

He is lying.

COUNT

You shall not escape the doom that
waits you.

AZUCENA

Oh, help.

COUNT

Now tie those ropes more tightly.
(The soldiers obey.)

AZUCENA

Oh, help me.

CHORUS

Let her howl.

AZUCENA

And you, my son Manrico, why do you
not come to help your mother; why
do you not come to help your poor
and helpless mother?

COUNT

Are you mother of Manrico?

FERRANDO

Tremble!

COUNT

Thank God! And in my power. O
thank God!

AZUCENA

Relent, and spare my sorry life;
Unloose these ropes that bind me.
This torment cuts me like a knife,
Yet puts all fear of death behind me.
Ungodly son of ghoulish father,
Fear the fate that waits you:
Tremble, for God will punish you—
For know, the hand of God is harsh on
those who kill.

COUNT

O shameless gipsy, do you ask me
To show you mercy,
When my vengeance waits for you.
The joy which now I feel is more
Than words of mine can say;
Full payment for the vile deed
That killed my brother shall I pay.
And all the grief which I have felt
Ah, yes, through you will be avenged.

FERRANDO AND CHORUS

Vile gipsy, soon the fire will rise,
You will see it rising for you.
Nor will that fearful torture
End the punishment for you:
Ah, no, for you wait the flames of Hell.
There you will burn,
There you will suffer,
And your soul will burn forever.
(At a sign from the Count, the soldiers
drag Azucena with them. They enter
the tent, followed by Ferrando.)

Scena 2

Sala adiacente alla capella in Castellor, con verone in fondo.

LEONORA

Quale d'armi fragore poc'anzi intesi?

MANRICO

Alto è il periglio! Vano dissimularlo
fora! Alla novella aurora assaliti sa-
remo.

LEONORA

Ahimè! Che dici?

MANRICO

Ma de' nostri nemici avrem vittoria.
Pari abbiamo al loro ardir, brando e
coraggio.

(*a Ruiz*) Tu va. Le belliche opre, nell'
assenza mia breve, a te commetto.
Che nulla manchi!   (*Ruiz parte.*)

LEONORA

Di qual tetra luce il nostro imen ri-
splende!

MANRICO

Il presagio funesto, deh, sperdi, o cara!

LEONORA

E il posso?

MANRICO

Amor, sublime amore,
In tal istante ti favella al core.
Ah! sì, ben mio; coll'essere
Io tuo, tu mia consorte,
Avrò più l'alma intrepida,
Il braccio avrò più forte.
Ma pur, se nella pagina
De' miei destini è scritto,
Ch'io resti fra le vittime,
Dal ferro ostil trafitto,
Fra quegli estremi aneliti,
A te, il pensier verrà,
E solo in ciel precederti,
La morte a me parrà!

(*Odesi il suono dell'organo dalla vicina cappella.*)

LEONORA E MANRICO

L'onda de' suoni mistici
Pura discenda al cor!
Vieni, ci schiude il tempio
Gioje di casto amor!

(*Mentre s'avviano giubilanti al tempio, Ruiz entra frettoloso.*)

RUIZ

Manrico!

MANRICO

Che?

RUIZ

La zingara, vieni, traceppi mira . . .?

MANRICO

Oh Dio!

RUIZ

Per man de' barbari accesa è già la
pira . . .

MANRICO (*accostandosi al verone*)

Oh ciel! mie membra oscillano—
Nube mi copre il ciglio!

LEONORA

Tu fremi!

MANRICO

E il deggio! Sappilo, io son . . .

LEONORA

Chi mai?

MANRICO

Suo figlio! Ah, vili! Il rio spettacolo
quasi il respir m'invola!
Raduna i nostri! Affrettati, Ruiz! Va,
torna, vola!

(*Ruiz parte.*)

Di quella pira l'orrendo foco
Tutte le fibre m'arse, avvampò!
Empii, spegnetela, o ch'io fra poco
Col sangue vostro la spegnerò.
Ero già figlio prima d'amarti,
Non può frenarmi il tuo martir . . .
Madre infelice, corro a salvarti,
O teco almeno corro a morir!

Scene II

A room next to the chapel in Castellor, with a balcony at the back. Manrico, Leonora, and Ruiz.

LEONORA

What's that clashing of arms outside the castle?

MANRICO

That means great danger. To deceive you would be foolish. Before the dawn of tomorrow we shall be assaulted.

LEONORA

Oh, no. That can't be.

MANRICO

But when we meet our foes we shall defeat them! They have strength, but we have right! And we have courage.

(to Ruiz) And you . . . As to the fighting, for a while what is needed I trust to you now. Leave nothing undone. *(Ruiz departs.)*

LEONORA

What a fearsome splendor is here to light our wedding.

MANRICO

No, you must forget such grim thoughts. You must, my dear one.

LEONORA

How can I?

MANRICO

To love, and to love's thriving,
Give your heart's passion, and your soul's deepest striving.
Ah, yes, beloved maid, the thought that you are mine forever,
New joyous strength to me has brought: triumph crowns endeavor.
But yet, if fighting I should fall,
By will of hostile destiny.
One thought, my dear, atones for all:
If I die, it is for thee.
And when my life shall fade away,
My prayer from earth to God shall be:
With you until eternity,
In heaven's eternal day.
(The sound of an organ is heard from the nearby chapel.)

LEONORA AND MANRICO

The waves of sound bear mystic truth
That reaches deep into our hearts.
Now come: the altar opens to us
All the joys of lawful love.

(Ruiz enters hastily, just as they are joyously entering the chapel.)

RUIZ

Manrico!

MANRICO

What?

RUIZ

The gipsy woman, captured, and bound in fetters.

MANRICO

Oh God!

RUIZ

Already they have lit for her the fatal fire.

MANRICO

(rushing to the balcony)

Oh God, my God! What shall I do? My hands shake, my eyes are clouded.

LEONORA

You're trembling.

MANRICO

God help me. Do you know . . . I am . . .

LEONORA

Oh, speak!

MANRICO

. . . her son. Ah. Oh, vile ones, this sad, sad spectacle, the smoke, it chokes my breathing. Collect my forces; bestir yourself, Ruiz. Go. Go. Hurry.

(Ruiz departs.)

Sight of grim horror, fire high in full blaze.
My limbs are shivering, brain all a-craze.
Demon destroyers, fill me with cruel hate,
With blood fulfilling my vengeful fate.
Should not your true son come to redeem you,
Have strength to overcome every grim foe.
Oh my poor mother, I come to save you:
Yes, though the flames there swallow me too.

LEONORA

Non reggo a colpi tanto funesti . . .
Oh, quanto meglio saria morir!

(*Ruiz torna con armati.*)

RUIZ E ARMATI

All'armi, all'armi! Eccone presti
A pugnar teco, teco a morir!
(*Manrico parte, frettoloso, seguito da
Ruiz e dagli armati, mentre odesi
dall'interno fragor d'armi e di bel-
lici strumenti.*)

ATTO QUARTO

IL SUPPLIZIO

SCENA 1

*Un'ala del palazzo dell'Aliaferia: all'-
angelo una torre, con finestre assicu-
rate da spranghe di ferro.—Notte
oscurissima.*

*Si avanzano due persone ammantel-
late: sono Ruiz e Leonora.*

RUIZ (*sommessamente*)

Siam giunti; ecco la torre, ove di Stato
gemono i prigionieri. Ah, l'infelice
ivi fu tratto!

LEONORA

Vanne . . . Lasciami, nè timor di me ti
prenda. Salvarlo io potrò, forse.

(*Ruiz si allontana.*)

Timor di me? Sicura, presta è la mia
difesa!

(*I suoi occhi figgonsi ad una gemma
che la fregia la mano destra.*)

In questa oscura notte ravvolta, presso
a te son io, e tu nol sai!
Gemente aura, che intorno spiri, deh,
pietosa gli arreca i miei sospiri.
D'amor sull'ali rosee
Vanne, sospir dolente;
Del prigioniero misero
Conforta l'egra mente.
Com'aura di speranza
Aleggia in quella stanza;
Lo desta alle memorie,
Ai sogni dell'amor!
Ma, deh! non dirgli, improvvido,
Le pene del mio cor!

CORO

Miserere d'un'alma già vicina
Alla partenza che non ha ritorno;
Miserere di lei, bontà divina,
Preda non sia dell'infernal soggiorno.

LEONORA

Quel suon, quelle preci
Solenni, funeste,
Empiron quest'aere
Di cupo terror!
Contende l'ambascia,
Che tutta m'investe,
Al labbro il respiro,
I palpiti al cor!

MANRICO (*dalla torre*)

Ah! che la morte ognora
È tarda nel venir
A chi desia morir!

LEONORA

Oh ciel, sento mancarmi!

MANRICO

Addio, Leonora, addio!

LEONORA

Sull' orrida torre, ahi! par che la morte,
Con ali di tenebre librando si va!
Ah! forse dischiuse gli fian queste porte
Sol quando cadaver già freddo sarà!

MANRICO

Sconto col sangue mio
L'amor che posi in te!
Non ti scordar di me,
Leonora, addio!

LEONORA

Di te, di te scordarmi!

(*S'apre una porta; n'escono il Conte
ed alcuni seguaci.—Leonora è in
disparte.*)

CONTE (*ad alcuni seguaci*)

Udiste? Come albeggi, la scure al
figlio, ed alla madre il rogo.

(*Entrano i seguaci nella torre.*)

Abuso forse quel poter che pieno in me
trasmise il Prence! A tal mi traggi,

LEONORA

Against such blows no more can I
  struggle; oh, how much better for me
  to die!

(*Ruiz returns with soldiers.*)

RUIZ AND SOLDIERS

To arms now, to arms now.
See us now ready to fight on by your
  side, ready to die.

(*Manrico rushes out, followed by Ruiz
and the soldiers, while from within
is heard the clash of arms and
armor.*)

ACT IV
THE PUNISHMENT

SCENE I

*A wing of the palace of Aliaferia; in
the corner a tower with a window
secured with iron bars. Very dark
night. Two persons in cloaks come
forward: they are Leonora and Ruiz.*

RUIZ (*in a low voice*)

We're here now. There is the tower.
Deep in it are the prisoners Luna
captured. Poor doomed Manrico.
There he lies helpless.

LEONORA

Go now. Leave me here. Have no fear
about my safety. Perhaps I shall yet
save him.

(*Ruiz departs.*)

Why should I fear? Within this ring
is my sure protection. (*Her eyes are
fixed on a gem she wears on her right
hand.*)

Now gloom of night surrounds you. Yet
all unknown I am near you. Oh, my
Manrico. May gentle breezes, that
flow about me, to you now carry my
piteous sighing, my loving, piteous
sighing.
Love's tender wings I pray may bear
Prayers that my heart speaks bitterly.
Message of hope within my prayer—
Oh, may God help to set him free.
If hope has left him utterly,
Abandoned in his prison's gloom,
May love live again in his memory,
My true love to cheer his lonely room.
But if our ways should forever part,
He will not know the torment, the
  breaking of my heart.

WOMEN'S CHORUS

Miserere, for one already dying,
Starting the journey which has no
  returning.
Miserere, his soul to Heaven flying,
Saved through Thy grace from Hell's
  eternal burning.

LEONORA

What sound am I hearing,
Conveying such terror?
Grim shadows of horror
About me now cling.
What soul is thus fleeing
From life's bitt'rest part?
I cannot stop my trembling
I cannot control the wild pounding of
  my heart.

MANRICO (*in the tower*)

Ah, that death comes so slowly,
Though one for peace may cry,
Seeking with all his heart and soul only
  to die.

LEONORA

Oh God! How can I bear this?

MANRICO

Oh farewell, my Leonora, farewell.

LEONORA

From that fearful tower the horrible
  wings of Death
Now send forth their chilling power
  that freezes all breath.
Ah, never will he go through this dismal portal
Until as a corpse he is borne to his
  immortal
Rest: may God give peace to his soul.

MANRICO

Life ending in a grim cell,
Love that was vowed to thee;
Do not forget, my love,
The love I vowed to thee.

LEONORA

Manrico, do not forget me.

(*A door is opened; the Count and several of his followers come out.
Leonora goes to the side.*)

COUNT (*to his followers*)

Remember: take the axe to the son at
daybreak; bright fire for the mother.

(*The followers enter the tower.*)

I have no right to send these souls to
their death. The Prince gave me no

donna per me funesta!

Ov'ella è mai? Ripreso Castellor, di lei contezza non ebbi, e furo indarno tante ricerche e tante! Oh, dove sei, crudele?

LEONORA (*avanzandosi*)

A te davante.

CONTE

Qual voce, come! Tu, donna?

LEONORA

Il vedi.

CONTE

A che venisti?

LEONORA

Egli è già presso all'ora estrema, e tu lo chiedi?

CONTE

Osar potresti?

LEONORA

Ah, sì, per esso pietà domando!

CONTE

Che? tu deliri!
Io del rivale sentir pietà?

LEONORA

Clemente Nume a te l'ispiri.

CONTE

È sol vendetta mio Nume! Va!

(*Leonora si getta disperata ai suoi piedi.*)

LEONORA

Mira, di acerbe lagrime
Spargo al tuo piede un rio!
Non basta il pianto? svenami,
Ti bevi il sangue mio.
Calpesta il mio cadavere,
Ma salva il Trovator!

CONTE

Ah! dell'indegno rendere
Vorrei peggior la sorte,
Fra mille atroci spasimi
Centuplicar sua morte—
Più l'ami, e più terribile
Divampa il mio furor!

(*vuol partire*)

LEONORA

(*Si avviticchia ad esso.*)

Conte!

CONTE

Nè cessi?

LEONORA

Grazia!

CONTE

Prezzo non avvi alcuno ad ottenerla— scostati!

LEONORA

Uno ve n'ha, sol uno, ed io te l'offro.

CONTE

Spiegati, qual prezzo, di'?

LEONORA

(*stendendogli la destra con dolore*)

Me stessa!

CONTE

Ciel! tu dicesti?

LEONORA

E compiere saprò la mia promessa.

CONTE

È sogno il mio?

LEONORA

Dischiudimi la via fra quelle mura:
Ch'ei mi oda, che la vittima fugga,
e son tua.

CONTE

Lo giura?

LEONORA

Lo giuro a Dio, che l'anima tutta mi vede!

CONTE

Olà!

(*Si presenta un custode.—Mentre il Conte gli parla all'orecchio, Leonora sugge il veleno chiuso nell'anello.*)

LEONORA (*a parte*)

M'avrai, ma fredda, esanime spoglia.

CONTE (*tornando a Leonora*)

Colui vivrà.

such power. This woman drives me
into these acts of madness. Where
can she be now? Since the fall of
Castellor, no word has come to me
about her. My soldiers say the search
for her has been hopeless. Ah, cruel
one, where are you?

LEONORA *(coming forward)*

Here, now before you.

COUNT

That voice here! You here! My lady?

LEONORA

You see me.

COUNT

But why have you come here?

LEONORA

You surely know who dies this morning.
And yet you ask me.

COUNT

You dare to come here?

LEONORA

Ah yes, that I may receive the grace to
save him.

COUNT

Can you think that? Ah, should I
show mercy to my foe?

LEONORA

God grant that you be filled with
mercy.

COUNT

The God of vengeance now rules in my
heart. Go!
*(Leonora throws herself desperately at
his feet.)*

LEONORA

See where I shed these bitter tears:
At your feet I weep imploring.
If tears are not enough for you,
Then drink the blood from my heart
   pouring.
Trample my corpse on this cold floor,
But pardon the Trobador.

COUNT

Ah, willingly I would kill you.
Ten thousand tortures give you—
Pain greater than you've given me,
More than I'll give that vile one.
The more that you plead your love for
   him
The more burning grows my fury.
(He is about to leave.)

LEONORA *(clinging to him)*

Hear me.

COUNT

Not through yet?

LEONORA

Mercy.

COUNT

No price on earth could gain a pardon
for him. Try no more.

LEONORA

One price there is, one only. I offer
it to you.

COUNT

What's the price you're offering?
Speak!

LEONORA

*(extending her hands to him in her
grief)*
Myself.

COUNT

What? Do you mean it?

LEONORA

Whatever I may promise, that I will do.

COUNT

Can I be dreaming?

LEONORA

Now open wide the gates of yonder
prison, and let him in safety depart.
Then I am yours.

COUNT

You swear this?

LEONORA

I swear by God who protects every soul
in His world.

COUNT

Ho there!
*(A guard appears. While the Count is
speaking into the guard's ear, Leonora swallows the poison contained
in her ring.)*

LEONORA *(aside)*

I shall be yours, but not till I'm dying.
COUNT *(turning back to Leonora)*
Now he shall live!

LEONORA

(*da sè, alzando gli occhi, cui farme velo lagrime di gioia*)

Vivrà! Contende il giubilo
I detti a me, Signore,
Ma coi frequenti palpiti
Mercè ti rende il core!
Or il mio fine, impavida,
Piena di gioja attendo,
Potrò dirgli, morendo,
Salvo tu sei per me!

CONTE

Fra te che parli?
Volgimi, mi volgi il detto ancora,
O mi parra delirio . . .
Quanto ascoltai finora!
Tu mia, tu mia! ripetilo,
Il dubbio cor serena.
Ah! ch'io lo credo appena,
Udendolo da te!

LEONORA

Andiam!

CONTE

Giurasti! Pensaci!

LEONORA

È sacra la mia fè!

(*Entrano nella torre.*)

SCENA 2

Orrido carcere: in un canto finestra con inferriata: porta nel fondo: smorto fanale penedente dalla vôlta. Azucena giacente sovra rozza coltre; Manrico seduto a lei dappresso.

MANRICO

Madre, non dormi?

AZUCENA

L'invocai, più volte, ma fugge il sonno a queste luci! Prego.

MANRICO

L'aura fredda è molesta alle tue membra, forse?

AZUCENA

No; da questa tomba di vivi solo fuggir vorrei, perchè sento il respiro soffocarmi!

MANRICO (*torcendosi le mani*)

Fuggir!

AZUCENA

Non attristarti; far di me strazio non potranno i crudi!

MANRICO

Ahi, come?

AZUCENA

Vedi? Le sue fosche impronte m'ha già segnato in fronte il dito della morte!

MANRICO

Ahi!

AZUCENA

Troveranno un cadavere muto, gelido! anzi uno scheletro!

MANRICO

Cessa!

AZUCENA

Non odi? gente appressa, . . . i carnefici son . . . vogliono al rogo trarmi! Difendi la tua madre!

MANRICO

Alcuno, ti rassicura, qui non volge.

AZUCENA

Il rogo! Parola orrenda!

MANRICO

Oh, madre! oh, madre!

AZUCENA

Un giorno turba feroce l'ava tua condusse al rogo! Mira la terribil vampa! Ella n'è tocca già! Già l'arso crine al ciel manda faville;
Osserva le pupille fuor dell'orbita loro! Ahi, chi mi toglie a spettacol sì atroce!

(*cadendo tutta convulsa tra le braccia di Manrico*)

MANRICO

Se m'ami ancor, se voce di figlio ha possa di una madre in seno, ai terrori dell'alma oblio cerca nel sonno, e posa e calma.

(*La conduce presso alla coltre.*)

LEONORA

(*to herself, raising her eyes, which gleam with tears of joy*)
He lives! Then you have made my soul
Rejoice with rapture swelling.
I feel that my heart thrills and throbs
As though to burst its dwelling.
Now Death awaits impatiently,
But joy is there attending;
For now my dying breath
Will breath of life to him be sending.

COUNT

What words are these?
Turn back to me, with sounds once
  more caressing.
My soul was filled with wild joy
By your gift that brings a blessing:
You're mine, all mine!
Such ecstasy was never brought before
me.
Ah, that I could believe this—
That I shall have such bliss.

LEONORA

Now come.

COUNT

You've sworn it—remember that.

LEONORA

Ah, sacred is my oath.
(*They enter the tower.*)

SCENE II

A dismal dungeon. In a corner, a barred window; a door at the back; a dim lantern hanging from the wall. Azucena is lying on a rough pallet. Manrico sits near her.

MANRICO

Sleep now, dear mother.

AZUCENA

For my weary spirit vainly I seek peace
and rest in slumber. Help me.

MANRICO

Ah, the air here is cold, and perhaps
it weakens you.

AZUCENA

No. But from this tomb of the living I
long to be set free. Perhaps that is
why I suffocate here.

MANRICO (*wringing his hands*)
Escape!

AZUCENA

No, be not troubled. They cannot hurt
me, not with all their torments.

MANRICO

Why is that?

AZUCENA

See this! Do you see it written, where
all may read it plainly, that Death
has set his token?

MANRICO

Ah!

AZUCENA

They shall find me nothing but a
corpse, silent, stiffened, stark as a
skeleton.

MANRICO

No, no.

AZUCENA

You hear them? They're approaching
. . . the executioners . . . to take me
out and burn me. Protect your old
mother!

MANRICO

Ah mother, do not be frightened, for no
one will come to take you.

AZUCENA

The burning, the burning . . . Oh, how
I dread that.

MANRICO

Oh mother, poor mother.

AZUCENA

They dragged her, that mob so brutal
. . . my poor mother, they took her
to burn there. See where the flames
are leaping. They are already near
her. Her hair is burning; the sparks
fly to Heaven. Her eyes are wildly
staring, as the fierce flames embrace
her. Ah, what demon makes me see
this sight so atrocious!
(*Overwrought, she falls into Manrico's arms.*)

MANRICO

If you will heed the voice of your son,
a son who loves his mother dearly,
put this terror from your mind, and
look for peace now in slumber, to
soothe you and rest you.

(*He leads her back to her bed.*)

AZUCENA

Sì, la stanchezza m'opprime, o figlio.
Alla quiete io chiudo il ciglio,
Ma se del rogo arder si veda
L'orrida fiamma, destami allor!

MANRICO

Riposa, o madre, Iddio conceda
Men tristi immagini al tuo sopor.
   AZUCENA (*tra il sonno e la veglia*)
Ai nostri monti ritorneremo,
L'antica pace ivi godremo!
Tu canterai, sul tuo liuto,
In sonno placido io dormirò.

MANRICO

Riposa, o madre, io prono e muto
La mente al cielo rivolgerò.

AZUCENA

Tu canterai, sul tuo liuto,
In sonno placido ir dormirò.

MANRICO

La mente al cielo rivolgerò.
(*Azucena si addormenta; Manrico resta
   genuflesso accanto a lei.*)
(*S' apre la porta. Entra Leonora.*)

MANRICO

Che! Non m'inganno! Quel fioco lume?

LEONORA

Son io, Manrico!

MANRICO

Oh, mia Leonora!
Oh, mi concedi, pietoso Nume,
Gioja sì grande, anzi ch'io mora?

LEONORA

Tu non morrai, vengo a salvarti!

MANRICO

Come! A salvarmi? fia vero?

LEONORA

(*accennandogli la porta*)
Addio! Tronca ogn' indugio! t'affretta!
parti!

MANRICO

E tu non vieni?

LEONORA

Restar degg'io!

MANRICO

Restar!

LEONORA

Deh! fuggi!

MANRICO

No!

LEONORA

Guai! se tardi!
   (*cercando di trarlo verso l'uscio*)

MANRICO

No!

LEONORA

La tua vita!

MANRICO

Io la disprezzo!
Pur! Figgi, o donna, in me gli sguardi!
Da chi l'avesti? ed a qual prezzo?
Parlar non vuoi? Balen tremendo!
Dal mio rivale! Intendo, intendo!
Ha quest'infame l'amor venduto,
Venduto un core che mio giurò!

LEONORA

Oh, come l'ira ti rende cieco!
Oh, quanto ingiusto, crudel sei meco!
T'arrendi, fuggi, o sei perduto!
Nemmeno il cielo salvar ti può!

(*Leonora è caduta ai piedi di Manrico.*)

AZUCENA (*dormendo*)

Ai nostri monti ritorneremo,
L'antica pace ivi godremo,
Tu suonerai sul tuo liuto,
In sonno placido io dormirò!

AZUCENA

Yes, I shall look for some peace in slumber;
So may I find rest from woes without number.
But if you see again flames leaping bright,
Wake me so I may go, head held upright.

MANRICO

Sleep now, my mother, and leave these sad thoughts;
Let Heaven now bless and give you sweet rest.

AZUCENA

(*between sleeping and waking*)

Home to our mountains let our feet turn once more,
Peace ever seeking, weary and heartsore.
Stroke your sweet lute again, sing to it merrily;
Rest then will come to me from endless pain.

MANRICO

Rest you, dear mother, I'll kneel in prayer
That God give you peace, sweet rest from all care.

AZUCENA

You'll stroke your lute and sing to it sweetly,
Slumber will come and eternal rest.

MANRICO

May Heaven hear thy plea and weep for thee.

(*Manrico remains kneeling beside his mother as she falls into slumber. The door opens; Leonora enters.*)

MANRICO

God! Who is this? Do my eyes deceive me?

LEONORA

It's I, Manrico!

MANRICO

My Leonora. Oh, kind Heaven, endless thanks do I give you, that you send me this joy—seeing you before I die.

LEONORA

You will not die. I come to save you!

MANRICO

What's this? Come to save me? Is this true?

LEONORA

Farewell. Without delay you must go! Hurry!

(*pointing to the door*)

MANRICO

And will you follow?

LEONORA

No, no. I must stay.

MANRICO

You stay?

LEONORA

Go. Hurry.

MANRICO

No!

LEONORA

(*trying to pull him to the door*)
If you linger, then your life will . . .

MANRICO

No!

LEONORA

Ah, your safety!

MANRICO

No, I despise it.
Now Leonora, look in my eyes.
And tell the price you paid that you might save me.
You do not speak? Your face betrays you.
Is it my rival you're flaunting
Before me? Ah, such a crime
Against love's past believing!

LEONORA

Oh, how your wrath has made you blind.
Oh, how unjust, how cruel you are.
Do not stay, you must flee;
Not even Heaven could save you now.

(*Leonora falls at Manrico's feet.*)

AZUCENA (*in her slumber*)

Home to our mountains let our feet turn once more,
Peace ever seeking, weary and heartsore.
Stroke your sweet lute again, sing to it merrily—
Rest then will come to me from endless pain.

MANRICO

Ti scosta!

LEONORA

Non respingermi! Vedi? Languente,
oppressa io manco!

MANRICO

Va! Ti abbomino! Ti maledico!

LEONORA

Ah, cessa! Non imprecar; di volgere
per me la prece a Dio è questa l'ora!

MANRICO

Un brivido corse nel petto mio!

LEONORA

Manrico!

(Cade boccone.)

MANRICO

(accorrendo a sollevarla)

Donna, svelami—narra.

LEONORA

Ho la morte in seno.

MANRICO

La morte!

LEONORA

Ah, fu più rapida la forza del veleno
ch'io non pensava!

MANRICO

Oh, fulmine!

LEONORA

Senti . . . la mano è gelo,
Ma qui, qui foco terribil arde!

(toccandosi il petto)

MANRICO

Che festi, oh, cielo!

LEONORA

Prime che d'altri vivere
Io volli tua morir!

MANRICO

Insano! ed io quest'angelo
Osava maledir!

LEONORA

Più non resisto!

MANRICO

Ahi, misera!

(Entra il Conte, arrestandosi sulla
soglia.)

LEONORA

Ecco l'istante! io moro, Manrico! Or la
tua grazia, Padre del cielo, imploro!

MANRICO

Insano! ed io quest'angelo
Osava maledir!

LEONORA

Prima che d'altri vivere,
Io volli tua morir!

(spira)

CONTE

Ah! volle me deludere, e per costui
morir! Sia tratto al ceppo!

(indicando agli armati Manrico)

MANRICO

Madre! Oh, madre, addio!

(Parte fra gli armati.)

AZUCENA

(destandosi)

Manrico! Ov'è mio figlio?

CONTE

A morte corre!

AZUCENA

Ah ferma! M'odi!

CONTE

(trascinando Azucena presso la finestra)

Vedi!

AZUCENA

Cielo!

CONTE

È spento!

AZUCENA

Egl'era tuo fratello!

CONTE

Ei! quale orror!

AZUCENA

Sei vendicata, o madre!

(Cade a piè della finestra.)

CONTE (inorridito)

E vivo ancor!

FINE DELL'OPERA.

MANRICO

Now you must go.

LEONORA

Do not drive me hence. Look at me,...
how weary, and faint with weakness.

MANRICO

Go! i hate you now. And I curse you.

LEONORA

Manrico, listen. Take back your curse.
Now rather pray to God that He may
save me from damnation.

MANRICO

Your words send a shudder that tears
my heartstrings.

LEONORA

(falling to the ground.)

Manrico!

MANRICO

(rushing to raise her)

Dear one, what have you done? Tell
me.

LEONORA

I bear death within me.

MANRICO

What, death?

LEONORA

Ah, ah, how rapidly it courses through
my veins . . . this death-dealing
poison!

MANRICO

Oh, agony!

LEONORA

Feel here, my hand, how icy. But here,
within me, a fire is burning.

(clasping her breast)

MANRICO

Oh God, where art Thou?

LEONORA

Rather than live without you, I have
chosen, I have willed to die.

MANRICO

O madman, that I have cursed this
angel who is blest by God.

LEONORA

My hour has come.

MANRICO

O piteous one.

(The Count enters and pauses on the
threshold.)

LEONORA

I can endure no more. I die, Manrico.
Now grant me mercy, Father Who
art in Heaven.

MANRICO

O madman, that I have cursed this
angel who is blest by God.

LEONORA

Rather than live without you, I have
chosen, I have willed to die.

(She dies.)

COUNT

Ah. Then she wished to deceive me,
and for him she chose to die.
Now take him out!

(indicating Manrico to the soldiers)

MANRICO

Mother, farewell, my mother.

(He leaves, accompanied by the
soldiers.)

AZUCENA (awaking)

Manrico! Where do you take him?

COUNT

He meets his death now.

AZUCENA

You must not! Hear me!

COUNT

(dragging Azucena to the window)

Look there!

AZUCENA

Heaven!

COUNT

He dies!

AZUCENA

Then you have killed your brother.

COUNT

God! What have I done!

AZUCENA

You are avenged, my mother!

(She falls near the window.)

COUNT (in horror)

And I live on!

END OF THE OPERA